Ages 3+

Trace with Me

First Words

Trace the word to complete the

The _____ bee _____ is

bike

bike   bike

My dog is _____ bi

bike   bike

bik

Thinking Kids®
Carson-Dellosa Publishing LLC
Greensboro, North Carolina

Thinking Kids®
Carson-Dellosa Publishing LLC
PO Box 35665
Greensboro, NC 27425 USA

ISBN 978-1-4838-4588-3

apple	bug	dog	leg	rug
arm	bus	doll	little	run
baby	cake	drum	man	sad
ball	can	egg	milk	school
balloon	cap	farm	mittens	shoes
bat	car	foot	mom	short
bear	cat	fish	moon	sing
bed	chair	fork	mouse	sister
bee	cheese	frog	night	snake
big	chicken	girl	orange	spoon
bike	clock	hand	over	store
bird	clothes	happy	pen	sun
block	coat	hat	pencil	swim
boat	cold	hen	pet	table
book	cook	horse	pig	tall
bowl	corn	hot	plane	toy
box	cow	house	rabbit	train
boy	cup	jar	rain	tree
bread	dad	jump	rat	truck
brother	dish	kite	ring	under

ball

ball   ball

ball   ball

bat bat

bat bat

car

car   car

car   car

man

man   man

man   man

COW

COW   COW

COW   COW

tree

tree   tree

tree   tree

mom

mom mom

mom mom

dad

dad   dad

dad   dad

toy

toy toy

toy toy

bee

bee   bee

bee   bee

can

can   can

can   can

rug

rug   rug

rug   rug

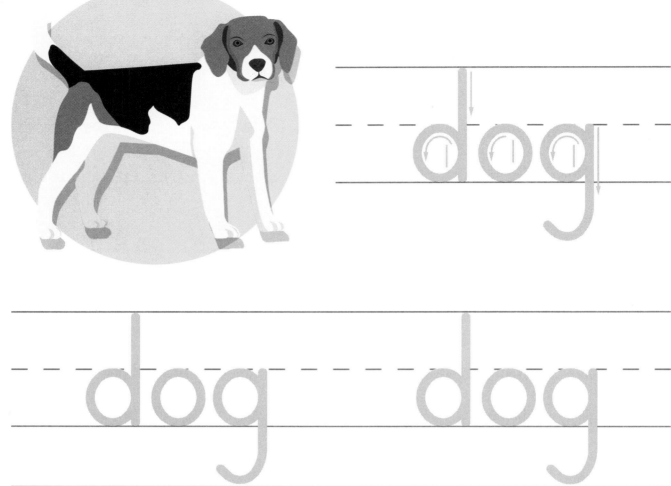

dog

dog   dog

dog   dog

cat   cat

cat   cat

pet

pet   pet

pet   pet

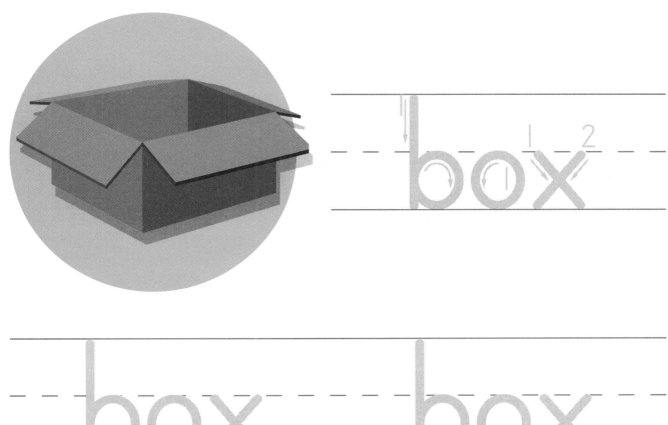

box

box   box

box   box

arm

arm   arm

arm   arm

leg

leg   leg

leg   leg

bed

bed   bed

bed   bed

hen

hen   hen

hen   hen

bug

bug   bug

bug   bug

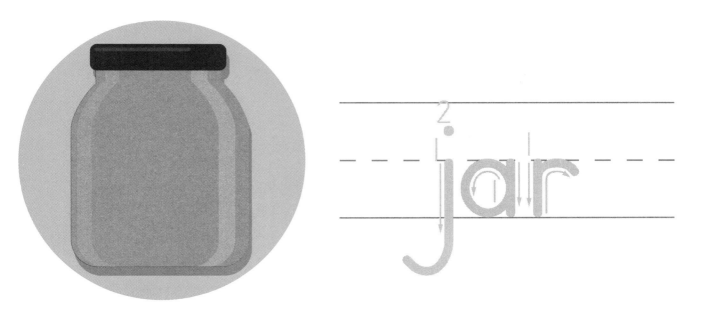

jar

jar   jar

jar   jar

cap

cap   cap

cap   cap

hat

hat   hat

hat   hat

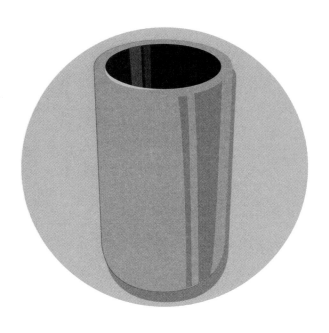

cup

cup   cup

cup   cup

pig

pig　　pig

pig　　pig

hot   hot

hot   hot

cold

cold   cold

cold   cold

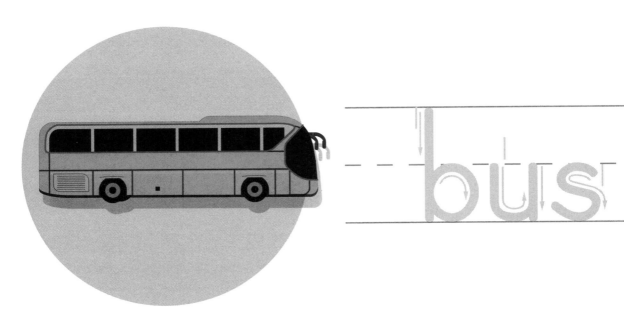

bus   bus

bus   bus

ring

ring   ring

ring   ring

egg   egg

egg   egg

milk

milk   milk

milk   milk

bear

bear   bear

bear   bear

fish

fish   fish

fish   fish

foot   foot

foot   foot

hand

hand   hand

hand   hand

doll

doll   doll

doll   doll

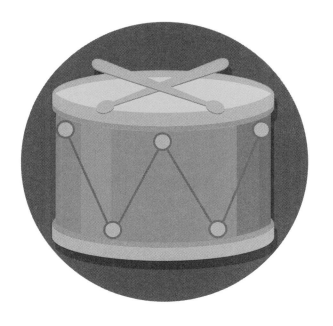

drum

drum drum

drum drum

bike

bike   bike

bike   bike

frog

frog   frog

frog   frog

boy

boy   boy

boy   boy

girl

girl girl

girl girl

dish

dish   dish

dish   dish

bird

bird   bird

bird   bird

sun

sun   sun

sun   sun

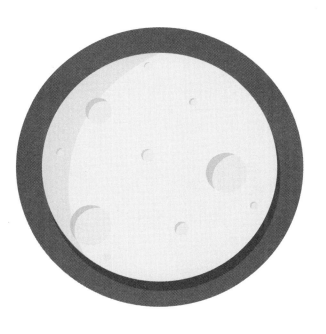

moon

moon moon

moon moon

book

book   book

book   book

coat coat

coat coat

cake

cake   cake

cake   cake

corn

corn corn

corn corn

run

run   run

run   run

jump

jump   jump

jump   jump

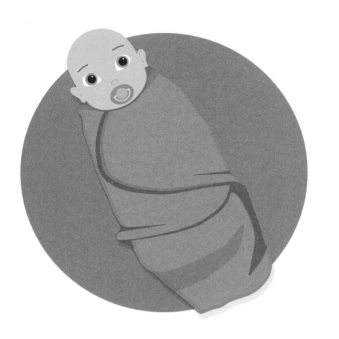

baby

baby baby

baby baby

farm

farm farm

farm farm

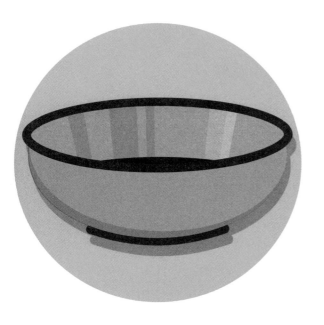

bowl

bowl   bowl

bowl   bowl

boat

boat boat

boat boat

sing

sing   sing

sing   sing

cook

cook   cook

cook   cook

rain

rain   rain

rain   rain

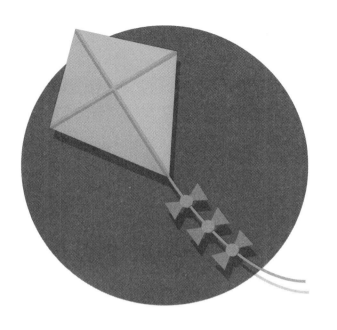

kite

kite   kite

kite   kite

swim

swim swim

swim swim

house

house house

house house

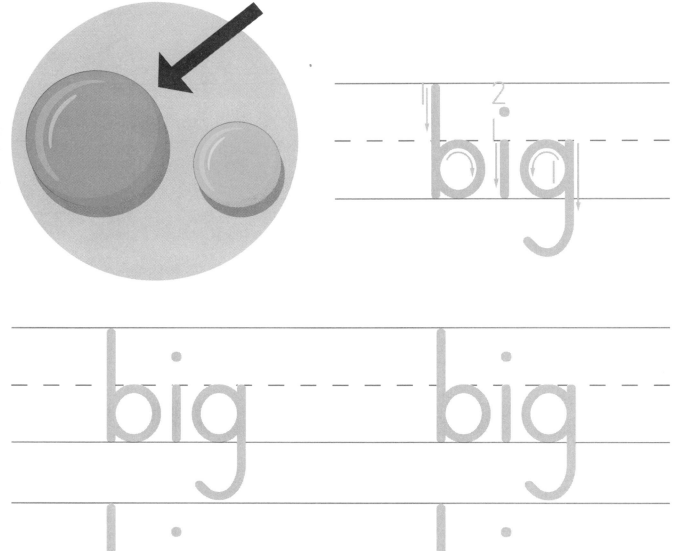

big   big

big   big

little

little   little

little   little

truck

truck truck

truck truck

orange

orange

orange

sad

sad   sad

sad   sad

happy

happy happy

happy happy

table

table   table

table   table

chair

chair chair

chair chair

clock

clock   clock

clock   clock

bread

bread bread

bread bread

train

train train

train train

apple

apple apple

apple apple

tall

tall   tall

tall   tall

short

short short

short short

block

block block

block block

horse

horse horse

horse horse

store

store store

store store

night

night   night

night   night

fork

fork   fork

fork   fork

spoon

spoon spoon

spoon spoon

snake

snake snake

snake snake

rat

rat   rat

rat   rat

mouse

mouse

mouse

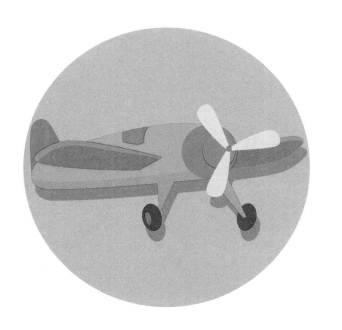

plane

plane plane

plane plane

over

over   over

over   over

under

under under

under under

shoes

shoes shoes

shoes shoes

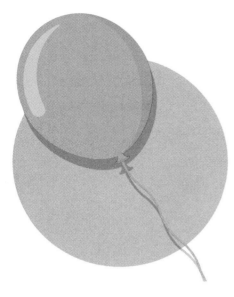

balloon

balloon

balloon

pen

pen   pen

pen   pen

pencil

pencil pencil

pencil pencil

cheese

cheese

cheese

mittens

mittens

mittens

sister

sister sister

sister sister

brother

brother

brother

chicken

chicken

chicken

school

school school

school school

rabbit

rabbit rabbit

rabbit rabbit

clothes

clothes

clothes

Trace the word to complete the sentence.

The _____apple_____ is red.

My _____arm_____ is long.

The _____baby_____ is big.

The _____ball_____ is round.

Trace the word to complete the sentence.

The __balloon__ is up.

My __bat__ is long.

The __bear__ is black.

The __bed__ is soft.

Trace the word to complete the sentence.

The ___bee___ is yellow.

My dog is ___big___.

The ___bike___ is blue.

The ___bird___ is red.

Trace the word to complete the sentence.

The ___block___ is green.

My ___boat___ is wet.

The ___book___ is short.

The ___bowl___ is round.

Trace the word to complete the sentence.

The ___box___ is big.

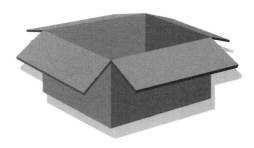

The ___boy___ is happy.

The ___bread___ is tasty.

My ___brother___ is funny.

Trace the word to complete the sentence.

The _bug_ is black.

My _bus_ is late.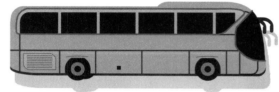

The _cake_ is round.

The _can_ is cold.

Trace the word to complete the sentence.

The ___cap___ is warm.

My ___car___ is white.

The ___cat___ is fluffy.

The ___chair___ is hard.

Trace the word to complete the sentence.

The _cheese_ is yellow.

The _chicken_ is loud.

The _clock_ is round.

My _clothes_ are on.

Trace the word to complete the sentence.

The _coat_ is warm.

My food is _cold_.

The _cook_ is working.

The _corn_ is good.

Trace the word to complete the sentence.

The _____cow_____ is eating.

My _____cup_____ is lost.

My _____dad_____ is nice.

The _____dish_____ is clean.

Trace the word to complete the sentence.

The ____dog____ is hungry.

My ____doll____ is pretty.

The ____drum____ is loud.

The ____egg____ is round.

Trace the word to complete the sentence.

The  is busy.

My ___foot___ is bare.

The ___fish___ is swimming.

The ___fork___ is silver.

Trace the word to complete the sentence.

The __frog__ is green.

The __girl__ is sad.

My __hand__ is little.

The boy is __happy__.

Trace the word to complete the sentence.

The ___hat___ is black.

The ___hen___ is white.

The ___horse___ is fast.

The pan is ___hot___.

Trace the word to complete the sentence.

My _house_ is blue.

The _jar_ is open.

The girl can _jump_.

The _kite_ is up.

Trace the word to complete the sentence.

My ̲l̲e̲g̲ is long.

My cat is ̲l̲i̲t̲t̲l̲e̲.

The ̲m̲a̲n̲ is eating.

The ̲m̲i̲l̲k̲ is white.

MILK

Trace the word to complete the sentence.

The ___mittens___ are warm.

My ___mom___ is funny.

The ___moon___ is white.

The ___mouse___ is little.

Trace the word to complete the sentence.

The __night__ is black.

My __orange__ is tasty.

The cow is __over__ the moon.

The __pen__ is lost.

Trace the word to complete the sentence.

The _pencil_ is yellow.

My _pet_ is sick.

The _pig_ is clean.

The _plane_ is fast.

Trace the word to complete the sentence.

My _____rabbit_____ is white.

The _____rain_____ is wet.

The _____rat_____ is gray.

The _____ring_____ is pretty.

Trace the word to complete the sentence.

The _____ rug _____ is long.

I can _____ run _____ fast.

The boy is _____ sad _____.

The _____ school _____ is busy.

Trace the word to complete the sentence.

The _____shoes_____ are brown.

My bed is _____short_____.

I can _____sing_____ songs.

My _____sister_____ is fun.

Trace the word to complete the sentence.

The _snake_ is fast.

My _spoon_ is lost.

Penny's Pets

The _store_ is big.

The _sun_ is hot.

Trace the word to complete the sentence.

I can ___swim___ today.

The ___table___ is high.

She is ___tall___.

The ___toy___ is fun.

Trace the word to complete the sentence.

The ___train___ is long.

The ___tree___ is green.

The ___truck___ is heavy.

The bug is ___under___ a leaf.